Learning to Let Go

Embrace Freedom, Find Peace, and Transform Your Life

Mary L. Cody

Table of contents

Introduction

Letting go of the past is not always simple. Sadly, every one of us deals with challenging circumstances and problems in life that could make it difficult to let go and proceed with our lives. Some such instances include letting go of a prior relationship, struggling to accept our upbringing, and learning to forgive others.

We find it difficult to let go of the past since some unresolved emotions have to be taken care of. We cannot proceed until these feelings are under control.

Finding the core feeling or emotions you are experiencing and knowing what they are trying to say to you is the first step in letting go. Basic information about our surroundings and ourselves comes from our emotions.

One or more of the following key emotions will probably help one to understand why one finds it difficult to let go of the past: guilt, regret, sadness, or anger. Guilt is a feeling that alerts us to having broken some rule or convention. "I should have done this," for instance, or "Why did I do that?" Regret shares our yearning that things from the past may have been different. Finally, fury is a feeling that indicates we sense something is unfair or wrong. Anger can also be connected to melancholy since it results from feeling wounded. Unresolving these feelings will make it difficult to live in the present and advance.

If your feelings are guilt, then grow from the past to avoid repeating it. We get guilty for this reason. If you can, second, pay reparations. If you have had a falling-out with a family member due to different arguments, for instance, learn to validate people and use more efficient communication instead of assuming personal responsibility by letting go. Then start the first step and call the family member to mend the bond. Should they not show a positive response, you have done all you could and have nothing to feel bad about now.

Look out for unhelpful thinking, too. Look at the data for and against the way you view yourself if you feel as though a past event makes you "bad, rotten, inadequate, or inferior."

Do not let one unfortunate event define who you are as a person.

Should you experience remorse, name what it is. Go out and start doing it now. If you have been regretful for many years, you will feel regretful some years later if you do not step out and act! Here are several instances:

If you have unresolved business, get to it. Look at what is still to be done; if necessary, start from the beginning and carry on where you left off.

If you intend to do something, go out and accomplish it. Go out and pick some dance lessons and go dancing with pals if your parents never let you dance.

Learn to be forceful if your life has been meek and unassuming and if you have not voiced your wants and ideas.

Write a letter expressing how you feel, and then read it to a loved one who you regret not telling that you loved them and they have passed on.

Determine your desired difference and then progressively implement those adjustments.

Change your behavior if you believe you have mistreated someone and have damaged them. Perhaps the part about overcoming guilt will also be useful.

Ask yourself the following questions if you find yourself struggling with regrets since you believe you made the wrong choice: these could also be of use should you additionally be feeling guilty:

Was the decision I took the best one I could have taken right then?

Are any of the benefits resulting from prior decisions or events discounted by me?

Am I only concentrating today on the negative aspects?

Did I know what I know "now," "then"?

Chances are you might have considered over and over a former event or choice and hence have fresh ideas. But since you lacked these insights in the past, is it fair to criticize yourself today?

Was my influence over the circumstance or incident rather limited?

What are the advantages and disadvantages of retaining your rage?

Do you still have pain? Is the other individual?

Let go of it if you think the cost is too high, and if you need assistance, employ visualization.

The choice to let go is entirely yours. People often find it difficult to let go because they believe that doing so invalidates their experiences or implies that the hurt or wrong they suffered was meaningless. This viewpoint is wholly false. For instance, if someone were to let go of the past and accept that the people who mistreated and neglected them as children were justified, it does not imply that the events were inconsequential. Neglect and abuse are never acceptable. On the other hand, clinging to the emotions will only prolong the sufferer's suffering. Learn to let go gradually, even when it's tough. Well lived is the best retaliation! Try not to worry about the past and do what was taken from you, if at all possible. For instance, go out and take some classes to learn how to paint if your parents forbade you from doing so.

It can be beneficial to try to comprehend why someone injured you. Did they truly intend to do this?

Are there any other relevant circumstances?

Depending on the circumstances, understanding the reasoning behind someone's behavior might assist in easing hurt and resentment. Write a letter expressing your feelings if the occasion or the individual are no longer with us. Try to come to a resolution about it. You might decide to burn the letter, tear it up, or perform some other ritual or significant action that will help you come to terms with the past.

Chapter 1

When you have a tough time, fail, or find anything you don't like about yourself, self-compassion is responding in the same sympathetic and understanding manner you would with a good friend. Self-compassion consists of three elements: mindfulness against over-identification, common humanity against isolation, and self-kindness against self-judging.

1. Awareness against over-identification

This is fundamental for self-compassion and offers the insight required to be with ourselves as we are and to validate our suffering. Steering clear of two common reactions to suffering—avoidance and over-identification—this is a balanced condition.

2. Common Humanity Against Separation

> Common humanity is realizing that, rather than something that only "me" goes through, sorrow and personal inadequacy are inevitable aspects of the shared human experience.

3. Self-Kindness Against Self-judging

Self-compassion is essentially kindness— that is, a gentle and forgiving of ourselves when we fail, struggle, or feel inadequate rather than ignoring our suffering or punishing ourselves with self-criticism.

Self-compassion in daily life is realizing when we're struggling and instead of evaluating and berating ourselves, we treat our suffering with compassion and kindness—as we would a close friend. Research showing that emotional well-being depends on our relating to ourselves in a kind, pleasant way is currently really impressive and mounting. Though for many of us the first reaction is not self-compassion, this ability can be developed even for those of us who did not acquire it as children.

Chapter 2

Living successfully requires you to separate items worth worrying about from those not worth worrying about.

Some decisions are not up to you in life; some events you are not in charge of. Likewise, certain decisions you are in charge of and some things you are accountable for.

It is advisable to focus your efforts on making changes to the things that you can influence, accept responsibility for, and control.
Certain things are out of your hands, things you are not accountable for, and it would be silly to waste your time and energy attempting to change them. There are five

things in your control and three things outside your control:

Things In Your Control

1. Your judgment.

You may easily dispute with others' points of view, but you can also debate with yourself. You have the ability to examine your own ideas and reason your way to better decisions.

2. Your Impulses

You may be unable to control your knee-jerk reactions to a situation, which frequently last only a few seconds, but you always have the ability to develop patience or self-control in order to overcome your urges and make wiser decisions about how to proceed. It may not be easy, but it is definitely feasible and hence under your control.

3. Your desires

You could argue that people cannot control their wants, but this is not totally correct. Consider an extreme example: someone addicted to heroin. Even though the stirrings of want may be with them for the rest of their lives, they can replace this desire with an even stronger desire: the desire to get sober.

4. Your Aversions.

Anxiety and anxiety are sometimes exacerbated when the thing one fears is avoided. When faced with such terror, one's emotions will drive them to avoid the source of the fear. However, we can overcome this aversion and confront what we dread. This process is a key pillar of personal development.

5. Your mental faculties

If we discover that we lack in some mental area, we have the ability to change and learn. This is the essence of "self-improvement." If we put in enough effort to improve our mental faculties, astonishing transformations can happen.

Things Outside Your Control

1. Your Body. You may improve your dietary preferences, increase your motivation to exercise, and overcome your aversions to healthy eating. However, you have no direct control on your genetics, height, eye color, bone structure, bone density, immune system, susceptibility to illness, or risk of injury or death.

2. Material possessions. You have the ability to read money-making books, cultivate the drive to labor more, and strengthen your mental faculties, all of

which raise your chances of earning more material belongings. Despite all of this, you may still fail. Your assets may be taken away, and your belongings stolen. There are numerous events that could occur outside of your control that could impede your efforts to acquire or preserve material assets.

3. Other People's Views of You

You have the ability to develop your social abilities and create judgments and wants that will help you become more loved and respected, but this is ultimately beyond your direct control. The socioeconomic class into which you were born, the way you look, the tone of your voice, the person you're engaging with previous experiences, the amount of sleep they got, and a million other factors all influence how others view you.

Conceptualizing the Dichotomy of Control

When it comes to understanding The Dichotomy of Control, it is important to note how much freedom you have in exercising what you can control. Your intentions and judgments are delightfully unfettered, unconstrained by anything. In contrast, results and reactions are fragile and weak.

For this reason, the intelligent person directs their efforts toward the open area over which they have direct control, rather than the inferior space over which they have no influence. That space is not their issue.

If you genuinely embrace this practice by realizing what belongs to you and what does not, you can expect:

* You will feel emancipated and free.
* You will not harbor anger or animosity in your   heart.
* Everything you do will be your choice.
* Nobody will have the power to harm you.

Your life will revolve solely around your actions and intentions, and nothing else will have any effect on you.

If you use the dichotomy of control poorly and confuse what is in your control for what is not, here's what

you   can   expect:

* You will live a life full of suffering and misery.
* You will be dissatisfied frequently.
* You will constantly strive for goals that you will never achieve.
* Others will have the ability to hurt you at any time.

The Right Intention to Practice the Dichotomy of Control

You have to practice religiously if you wish to get the great advantages The Dichotomy of Control offers. If you want great freedom and happiness, you must fundamentally change your life.

If you are practicing the dichotomy and

looking for riches and glory, you will probably fall short in both directions.

Spend some time alone examining the duality of control to reach degrees of personal liberation you never would have thought possible. Put yourself in a paradox of control training camp, so to speak, set aside all other objectives for a while.

Chapter 3

If you haven't noticed before, you will hear a "voice" in your head when you first start meditation. Not only does it talk to you, but it never stops. Starting from the time you wake up until you go to sleep, it talks nonstop. For some of us, it won't even stop there.

This voice is generally not very useful. It comments on our lives all day. It speculates. It likes and dislikes. It makes judgments about everything (he/she/I/life). It labels things. It complains. It compares us to everyone else. It worries and plans for the future. It keeps replaying and regretting the past. It creates stories about our life that frequently do not reflect our reality at all.

It accomplishes all of this swiftly and automatically, so our judgments about everything we experience can quickly become habitual, even automated. We often aren't even conscious we're doing it, but the constant flow of judgmental thoughts makes it impossible to attain inner calm.

How Judgmental Thinking Causes Suffering.

Our impression of life and our capacity to view things as they truly are can be much influenced by judgmental thinking. When we approach people or events with preconceptions or prejudices, we tend to filter data through these lenses, therefore distorting reality and perhaps causing misery in many forms.

First of all, judgmental thinking results from our natural inclination to classify and name objects according on our past experiences, views, and society expectations. This classification becomes problematic when it oversimplifies complicated reality, even although it can occasionally be useful for fast decisions. Saying someone as "lazy" or "incompetent," for instance, based on one incident of behavior misses the many elements impacting their behavior.

This kind of critical thinking locks us off from appreciating the subtleties of a situation or a person's motivations, therefore causing suffering. It generates divide and misinterpretation, so encouraging conflict rather than empathy and connection. Although we often feel superior or moral when we criticize others, this feeling is flimsy and might cover insecurities or concerns in ourselves.

Moreover, judgmental thinking clouds our view with prejudices, therefore preventing us from seeing things as they truly are. Events and actions are seen through a limited prism that supports rather than questions our preconceptions. This confirmation bias inhibits not only our personal development but also our capacity to change with fresh knowledge or viewpoints.

In interpersonal interactions, judgmental thinking creates obstacles in real connection and intimacy. We miss the special traits and contributions of people when we continually criticize or evaluate them. Loneliness, isolation, and a dearth of meaningful interactions can all follow from this.

Moreover, judgmental thinking goes beyond our contacts with others to how we view ourselves and our own experiences. We can criticize ourselves harshly depending on unrealistically high standards or make negative comparisons to others, which would cause low self-esteem or inadequacy.

One must develop mindfulness and self-awareness if one is to overcome judgmental thinking and the related pain. Mindfulness enables us to see our ideas and feelings without instantly reacting to them, thereby enabling us to challenge our assumptions and investigate several points of view. By means of empathy and compassion for others and ourselves, we foster openness and understanding instead of critique and separation.

Seeking many points of view and questioning our own presumptions also helps us to widen our horizons and lessen the effect of prejudice on our judgment. Curiosity and sincere interest in learning about the experiences of others might help to turn judgmental impulses into chances for development and communication.

Ultimately, judgmental thinking distorts our view of reality and prevents true interactions, therefore generating misery. Mindfulness, empathy, and a readiness to question our own prejudices can help us to see things as they truly are and lead to more peace and fulfillment in our life.

Why Our Mind Developed to Judge andCreate Meaning?

Why does our mind go through all the evaluating anyway? And why does it leap to judgments regarding the events around us so fast? Why does it start linking often useless stories to our experiences and resort to quick judgments? Like so many useless things the mind unintentionally performs, it is simply keeping you alive and safe; it has developed to serve and protect you. See the mind as your survival machine.

Your mind absorbs loads of sensory information in any one moment and must sift it all to emphasize what is most vital if you are to survive. The minds "filter" continuously asks these two fundamental questions to do this:
1) What does this mean?
2) What do I do?

Your mind wants to know exactly what's going on in your surroundings. 'What does it mean?' can alternatively be pronounced 'what is it?' - your mind tries to make any unknowns clear and understandable so that you know you're safe. It also wants you to respond fast to what you see, feel, and hear. When it asks 'What do I do?', it is determining if you should run, fight, or hide, or if you are   fine   and   safe.

When your mind is creating meanings and judgments about the objects around you--what they signify and what you should do--it wants to know what's going on as soon as possible: speed always beats accuracy! As a result, its decisions are best described as 'snap assessments'. They are quick, but not always accurate. In our ancestors' time, a delayed answer could have meant the difference between life and death if a wolf   was   in   the   woods!

However, having a wolf on your tail is unlikely in today's environment, when you are often relatively safe. Instead, imagine this more plausible scenario. You're in a parking lot with your grocery bags, headed towards your car, and just as you're about to step out from between two cars, another car races by, almost hitting you as you step out. It could have knocked you over, yet you remain unhurt, as the automobile continues on, far too quickly. Your body surges with adrenaline; you almost got hit by that car!

Your mind takes a brief snapshot of what is going on, scrambling to comprehend and make sense of what has just occurred. It sees two things: the automobile is a sleek, shining convertible, and the woman's reflection in the rear-view mirror shows that she wears luxury sunglasses and has salon-perfect hair. The mind immediately replies with the thought: 'Rich bitch!' This quick decision is typical of our instinctual thoughts.

The problem is that it's easy to start believing in that snap judgment and let it impact your ideas about other individuals. Perhaps you dislike other people who wear nice sunglasses or drive a sleek, beautiful car. When this happens, we can no longer 'see' the human being beyond their sunglasses or the vehicle they drive.

These quick judgments have the potential to color our view of the world and skew our perceptions, but we can untangle ourselves using the power of mindfulness and kindness.

Adopting A Beginner's Mind

Developing a 'beginner's mind' is an excellent approach to break free from the mind's judging inclinations. What do I mean by this? The beginner's mentality is simply one that suspends judgments.

A beginner's mentality is open and receptive, ready to try everything as if it were the first time. It does not judge or assume that it already knows better. The beginner's mind approaches life with an open mind, free of preconceived notions about what it should be.

This style of being reconnects us with a new way of seeing and allows us to actually be present in the most important times of our lives - and with the people we care about. Next time you want to judge what someone is saying, listen closely and maybe think to yourself, 'Hmm, isn't that interesting?' If you are open to learning something new, you may be surprised by what you discover!

This is where your beginner's mind can truly help you let go of your quick judgments about the people, places, and events in your life. When you face reality moment by moment, you let go of your connection to these judgmental viewpoints and embrace the openness of a beginner's mind.

Chapter 4

Humans do not only consider what is happening in our life here and now. We also have capacity for both the past and the future. Our perspective on the events in our lives reflects our feelings really closely. Studies have demonstrated that self-distance can enable us to consider past bad incidents in our life. Recent studies examined the impact of self-distancing in regards to a future one fears.

One useful psychological skill that helps people to see challenging past and future events from a different angle is self-distance. It's like seeing an experience or issue from a third-person viewpoint, as though you were an observer rather than a participant, mentally stepping back from it. This method helps to handle difficult life situations in numerous ways.

Self-distance helps one control emotions.

Strong emotions like regret, wrath, or anxiety can overwhelm us when we get overly attached to a challenging previous incident or worry too much about a future one. Mentally separating yourself helps us to build a psychological buffer that lets us view the matter more objectively. This detachment can enable better thinking and aid to lessen the intensity of unpleasant feelings. It improves cognitive functioning. Emotionally engaged in a situation might cause our ideas to be distorted by prejudices, presumptions, or spontaneous reactions. Backing off lets us examine the matter more logically, weigh other points of view, and come up with fresh ideas. When considering past errors or preparing for upcoming difficulties, this cognitive clarity is very helpful since it helps to solve problems more successfully and make decisions. It encourages self-examination and education. Seeing our experiences and ourselves from a distance helps us to assess our decisions, actions, and conduct more fairly. Through pattern recognition, strength identification, and areas for development, this introspection fosters personal development. By means of self-distancing, reflecting on

challenging previous events helps one to develop a better awareness of oneself and motivations, therefore fostering resilience and adaptation in the face of upcoming difficulties.

Self-distancing also helps one feel empowered and in control. Stepping back helps us to recover agency when faced with intense feelings or questions about the future. We grow more able to weigh several paths of action, create reasonable objectives, and design sensible plans. By encouraging a more positive attitude, this proactive method might help one overcome emotion of powerlessness or hopelessness.

Many methods can help one practice self-distancing: journaling from a third-person perspective, visualizing coaching a friend in a like circumstance, or using mindfulness techniques that promote detachment from instantaneous emotional reactions. These behaviors can become second nature with time, improving emotional well-being and resilience.

All things considered, self-distancing is a useful psychological tool for helping people examine unpleasant past events and get ready for present difficulties. Self-distancing helps one to grow and be resilient in negotiating the complexity of life by encouraging emotional control, improving cognitive processing, supporting self-reflection, and enabling proactive decision-making.

Chapter 5

When negativity surrounds you, it can seem impossible to break free. The truth is that no one deserves to be drawn into negativity, not even by themselves or others they love. Set boundaries first, and then try one of these ten techniques to break free from negativity.

There have been times in my life when I felt completely engulfed in a dark pool of pessimism. The water was occasionally laced with my hatred, jealousy, and suspicion. Sometimes the negative vibe was caused by my friends or relatives. Whoever is to blame doesn't always matter; once in the dark, it's easy to lose track of who is to blame. Especially if you're floating and have the option to exit the pool at any point.

Feelings are routines that develop with time. We have to start with our actions if we want to change how we feel. I talk a lot about how therapy helps me become a better version of myself. In addition to holding myself responsible, I hope to motivate anyone else who might be looking for a better way of life. One of my constant objectives is to overcome my own pessimism while negotiating other people's negativity, especially that of the people I love.

1. Run away as soon as you realize where the bad energy is coming from. or stroll. Or simply erect a fence.

2. Establish limits (even if the negative one is YOU). Establishing clear boundaries for what is and is not acceptable in your interactions and relationships is crucial. Talking about fictitious bad scenarios makes me anxious, therefore my family and

friends are aware that I will leave a conversation to protect myself.

3. Seek out points of light in the shadows. Everybody has unpleasant days occasionally, but those moments don't have to last forever. Try to find something happy in your surroundings if you feel like you're going in the wrong direction. Allow the glint to guide you toward optimism.

4. Jot down the positive aspects of life; this will help you remember them. Daily journaling can be challenging, but when the opportunity arises,

capture those moments of inspiration.

5. Give your bad memories a purposeful significance. This study is astounding, but there are a lot of positive benefits, such increased positive feeling, reduced symptoms of sadness, and a quicker recovery from stress—all of which contribute to resistance to adversity in the future. This is especially true if you can find meaning in prior negative occurrences.

6. Get moving and stand up. Were you aware that negativity adores sluggishness? Dance is my favorite way to move, so let it out.

7. Get outside and enjoy the many health advantages of being in nature.

8. Give up making oneself into victims. Everyone experiences bad things from time to time, and the more you complain about something, the more fuel you give the negative. Give up the victim mindset.

9. Reduce the amount of shit-talking and gossiping. This one can be challenging, but even hearing rumors about someone you don't know can make you feel depressed.

10. Attend to your own needs. Give importance to self-care practices that feed your soul. Love and care toward yourself, and never forget to celebrate each and every one of your

accomplishments, no matter how tiny they may appear.

Chapter 6

Developing a growth attitude is absolutely vital since it builds resilience, helps learning to flourish, and drives success. It helps you to see obstacles as chances, therefore enhancing your capacity for adaptation and problem-solving. Growth-oriented people realize they must push beyond their comfort zone, commit constant work, and grow from their mistakes if they are to reach their objectives. A growth mindset helps you to approach obstacles and disappointments differently, therefore increasing your degree of success and gratification. It's not only about your perspective; it's also about your behavior and response to the several circumstances life offers. A mindset oriented on learning and development can help you to recognize the possibility of improvement in every event.

Changing one's perspective can start a road trip both individually and professionally. A growth mindset helps you to gain the drive to reach for your dreams, the resilience to get back on track, and the power to go beyond challenges. A growth mentality helps you to prepare yourself to face the world unlike past times.

Recall, You Are on The Road of Growth.

Problems are chances for personal development. Like them. There is more than one ending for failure.

This is a teaching moment. Mastery is the road taken by effort. Encourage an abiding love of lifelong learning.

Find and value helpful criticism. Assemble people who motivate development around you.

Using these techniques can help you create conditions for unlimited development both personally and professionally. Recall that developing and maintaining a growth attitude requires work. Though it's not always simple, this trip is among the most fulfilling ones you might set off. So, inhale deeply, stretch outside your comfort zone, and enter the realm of development mindset. Your future self is grateful.

Conclusion

As we come to end this trip through the art of letting go, we have discovered the great force of letting go what no longer benefits us. Over these pages, we have explored the depths of human feeling, negotiated the complexity of relationships, and accepted the freeing power of surrender. Let's consider the main realizations that have brightened our road as we draw to a close this transforming inquiry.

Letting go is mostly about realizing that clinging to the past or to expectations simply makes us miserable. True freedom, as we have discovered, comes from releasing these weights—regrets, resentment, or fears—and allowing the current moment to bring opportunities. It's about acknowledging our experiences and choosing to proceed with clarity and intent, not about discounting or erasing them.

We have come across inspirational tales of people who have embraced the art of letting go with bravery and fortitude along our path. These tales have shown us that change is achievable when we trust in our own power and accept vulnerability—from letting go of poisonous relationships to renouncing the urge for control.

We do admit, though, that letting go is not always simple. It calls for self-compassion, tolerance, and a readiness to face unpleasantness. Unlearning past behaviors and ideas that no longer advance our development is a process. Let's keep in mind as we negotiate this process that every advance step—no matter how little—is evidence of our inner strength and ability for development.

Looking ahead, I motivate you to keep developing the habit of letting go in your daily life. Accept the ability of forgiveness—to yourself and others. Give up the demand for excellence and gracefully embrace the flaws of life. Release what no longer serves you to open room for fresh chances, relationships, and experiences to blossom.

I really thank you for joining me on this road as we separate ways. Your will to develop personally and your bravery to probe the depths of letting go are quite motivating. Recall that the path of letting go is one of constant progression toward more serenity, honesty, and fulfillment—not a destination. Always keep the lessons discovered here with you; the discipline of letting go will help you to find strength and comfort.

This last chapter seeks to highlight the main ideas, respect the difficulties, motivate the reader, and provide them with useful knowledge and support to use in their own life.

Having sincere hopes for your ongoing development and enjoyment,

MARY L. CODY